101 Money Mindset Prompts

A GUIDED WEALTH JOURNAL

101 Money Mindset Prompts

A GUIDED WEALTH JOURNAL

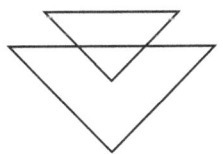

A LUXURY JOURNAL TO SHIFT HOW YOU THINK, SEE
AND REACT AROUND MONEY TO BUILD WEALTH HABITS.

CHRISTINA OSTROSKI

101 MONEY MINDSET PROMPTS : A GUIDED WEALTH JOURNAL

2025 ChristinaOstroski

Copyright © 2025 Christina Ostroski

All rights reserved. No part of this book may be reproduced, scanned, or distributed in any printed or electronic form without permission. No portion of this book may be used in any alternative manner whatsoever without express written consent from the publisher/author.

The author in this book has made every effort to ensure the accuracy of the information they have provided at the time of publication. The author does not assume and hereby disclaims any liability to any party for loss, damage, or disruption caused by errors or omissions, whether such errors or omissions were from accident, negligence, or any other cause. This book is not intended as legal, financial, or therapeutic advice. Always consult a qualified professional. This book is not a replacement for medical advice from a registered physician.

The publisher is not responsible for websites, social media, or other content that is not owned by the publisher.

ISBN Paperback: 978-1-0698303-0-2

@IAMCHRISTINAOSTROSKI

Christina
OSTROSKI

DEDICATION!

For the woman who knows she was made for more, wealth, power, and freedom. This is your space to remember who you are.

Christina O.

money mindset prompts

this book belongs to:

_____

Why THIS WORKS

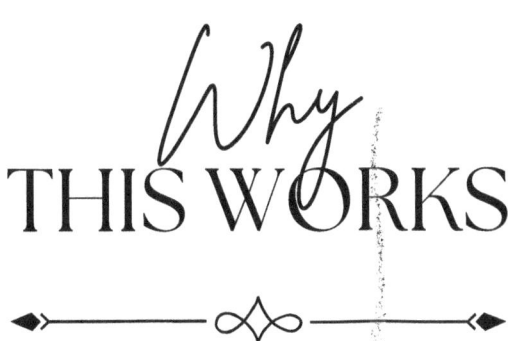

When you slow down and answer one powerful question a day, you rewire your mind. These prompts help you release old patterns and build new, empowering beliefs around wealth.

Every reflection strengthens your identity.
Every line you write becomes a declaration of who you're becoming.
The more you do it, the more wealth becomes your normal.

By committing to this journal daily, you'll start to shift how you think, feel, and respond to money.

These prompts are meant to help you build new beliefs, catch old thoughts, and create real alignment with wealth. Go one prompt at a time, stay consistent, and let your answers evolve with you.

Do one a day for 101 days and watch how your energy, habits, and results start to change.

YOUR NEXT EVOLUTION

Welcome to your next evolution.
This isn't just journaling. This is a daily activation — a conversation between you and the wealthiest version of yourself.
Every page holds a new perspective, a new energy, and a new identity waiting for you to step into.

HOW TO USE THIS BOOK

Give yourself a few quiet minutes each morning or night to get honest with your thoughts, shift your energy, and embody wealth one page at a time.

But if you're in flow , go for more.
There's no "wrong" pace here. This isn't about rules. It's about results.

Each page is simple:
- **Prompt** – The powerful question of the day.
- **Reflection** – Your space to write, feel, and uncover what's ready to shift.
- **Next Step** – Capture one inspired action or insight.

That's it. Clean. Transformational. Daily alignment with your wealth identity.

By committing to this journal daily, you'll start to shift how you think and respond to money.

This is where the magic begins. This It's a tool for transformation — a sacred practice of writing, feeling, and embodying the energy of wealth.

When you write, **feel** it.
When you visualize, **believe** it.
When you journal, **become** it.

Your words aren't just notes on paper; every line you write imprints new beliefs into your subconscious and programs your energy to match abundance.

Wealth Writing Method

- **Write as if it's already true:** "I am so happy and grateful now that money flows easily to me." Feel that in your body.

- **Visualize while you write:** Imagine what you're calling in. See it, hear it, sense it.

- **Journal from your higher self:** The version of you who already has it all — how does she think, speak, and feel? Write from that place.

- **Use prompts to access new levels:** Let each question open a doorway. Some days it'll feel deep, others light — both are powerful.

The more you connect to this energy, the faster you transform.

BEFORE YOU BEGIN

Before you dive in, capture where you are right now, your current money beliefs, emotions, and goals.

Use this space to write openly:

- How do I feel about money right now?
- What does wealth mean to me today?
- Where am I playing small with my finances or confidence?
- What would "wealthy me" believe instead?

You'll revisit these thoughts at the end in your **Final Wealth Check-In** and see your evolution on paper.

_____

_____

_____

_____

Wealth Notes

YOUR WEALTH ACTIVATION BEGINS HERE

This is where your relationship with money finlly starts to make sense. Every prompt helps you think, feel, and act like someone who actually keeps the wealth they create.

Wealth TRACKER

Use this tracker to mark your progress as you move through each wealth prompt. Watch your awareness, alignment, and confidence grow with every check mark.

PROMPT 1-25

Your Wealth Awareness Journey Begins

PROMPT 26-50

Keep Expanding Your Alignement

PROMPT 51-75

Deepen Your Confidence and Flow

PROMPT 76-101

Embody Wealth as Who You Are

FLOW

MOVE WITH TRUST, EASE, AND PRESENSE.

Prompt 1

Date: _____

What would I do if I trusted that money would always show up?

next steps

Move like money's guaranteed. Do one thing today from trust, not fear. Tonight, note how it showed up for you.

Prompt 2

Date: _____

How can I feel more connected to wealth today?

---

next steps

Do one thing that makes you feel good about money today.

Prompt 3

Date: _____

What does being confident with money look like for me?

---

next steps

Trust your own money decisions today

Prompt 4

Date: _____

How do I stay confident through financial changes?

next steps

When money changes, focus on what you can control. Your mindset, your effort, your plan.

Prompt 5

Date: _____

How can I show up today like money isn't a problem?

---

next steps

Make one choice today like you're not worried about money.

Prompt 6

Date: _____

What version of me attracts money easily?

next steps

Show up as her today. Speak, decide, and move like it's already working.

Prompt 7

Date: _____

What habits does my wealthy self have every day?

next steps

Pick one of those habits and start it right now.

Prompt 8

Date: _____

How can I act more like my richest self today?

next steps

Choose one thing she'd do and do it without hesitation.

Prompt 9

Date: _____

What mindset shift could help my money grow faster?

next steps

Catch one old thought and replace it with one that builds belief.

Prompt 10

Date: _____

What does a healthy money mindset look like in my day-to-day life?

next steps

Notice where you already think like a wealthy person and build on it.

Prompt 11

Date: _____

How do I stay positive when money feels uncertain?

next steps

List three things still working in your favor right now.

Prompt 12

Date: _____

How can I spend money in ways that match my values?

next steps

Buy with intention, not impulse. Let your money express what matters.

BELIEVE IN YOURSELF AND ALL THAT YOU ARE. KNOW THAT THERE IS SOMETHING INSIDE YOU THAT IS GREATER THAN ANY OBSTACLE. BELIEVE IN YOURSELF

Prompt 13

Date: _____

What would I do differently if I knew money was unlimited?

next steps

Take one bold move you'd normally hold back on.

Prompt 14

Date: _____

What money habit actually makes me happy?

next steps

Do more of that. It's proof you can enjoy money and grow it.

Prompt 15

Date: _____

What does "enough" really mean to me with money?

next steps

Define your enough. Write it, claim it, and stop moving the goalpost.

Prompt 16

Date: _____

How can I create more cash flow without pressure or stress?

next steps

Do one simple action that feels light but moves money closer.

Prompt 17

Date: _____

How can I notice abundance around me every day?

next steps

Find three signs of it today and say "thank you" out loud.

Prompt 18

Date: _____

How can I picture my financial goals clearly?

next steps

Write one goal in present tense and visualize it as already done.

Prompt 19

Date: _____

How can I practice daily gratitude for money?

next steps

Thank your money each time it moves — in or out.

Prompt 20

Date: _____

How does gratitude actually help me make more money?

next steps

Notice how good energy brings ideas, connections, and ease.

Prompt 21

Date: _____

How can I keep my momentum going with money?

next steps

Focus on progress, not perfection. One win at a time.

Prompt 22

Date: _____

How can I celebrate progress, even the small stuff?

next steps

Acknowledge one money win today, no matter how small.

Prompt 23

Date: _____

How does taking care of myself help me with money?

next steps

Do one thing today that refuels you. Energy makes you magnetic.

Prompt 24

Date: _____

How can I stay calm when money feels stressful?

next steps

Breathe, slow down, and remind yourself — you've handled worse.

Prompt 25

Date: _____

What five words describe my ideal money mindset?

next steps

Pick your five, write them somewhere you'll see every day.

Reflection
CHECK-IN #1

Take a minute to reflect on the last 25 prompts. What did you learn about yourself & your relationship with money?

WHAT'S YOUR FOCUS RIGHT NOW?

ACTION STEPS

1

2

3

REALIZATIONS

Wealth Notes

Wealth Notes

Wealth Notes

Wealth Notes

Wealth Notes

WEALTH

ALIGN HOW YOU THINK, FEEL, AND ACT WITH MONEY.

Prompt 26

Date: _____

What does wealth mean to me right now?

---

next steps

Write one sentence that defines wealth for you today.

Prompt 27

Date: _____

What does financial freedom mean to me?

---

next steps

Picture your life free from money stress and describe one detail of it.

Prompt 28

Date: _____

What does financial freedom let me do?

next steps

List three things you'd do if money wasn't holding you back.

Prompt 29

Date: _____

What's my biggest money dream right now?

next steps

Say it out loud like it's already yours.

Prompt 30

Date: _____

What money goal am I most excited about?

next steps

Write one small move you'll take toward it this week.

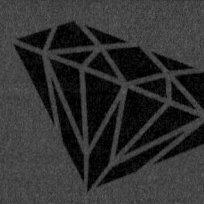

Prompt 31

Date: _____

How do I really feel about spending and saving?

next steps

Notice which one feels heavier and ask why.

Prompt 32

Date: _____

What money habits make me proud?

next steps

Celebrate one of them today.

Prompt 33

Date: _____

Which money goals actually match my purpose?

next steps

Circle the ones that feel meaningful, not just profitable.

Prompt 34

Date: _____

How can I make my money work harder for me?

next steps

Choose one simple way to grow or protect what you have.

Prompt 35

Date: _____

What does real wealth look like beyond cash?

next steps

Write down one non-money thing that makes you feel rich.

Prompt 36

Date: _____

What small daily moves help me build wealth?

next steps

Keep one of them going every day this week.

Prompt 37

Date: _____

How do I stay focused on long-term wealth?

next steps

Stop chasing quick wins. Keep your eyes on the bigger picture.

Reminder

YOU ARE CLOSER THAN YOU THINK

Christina Ostroski

Prompt 38

Date: _____

What money boundary do I need to set?

next steps

Decide where to say no — and hold that line.

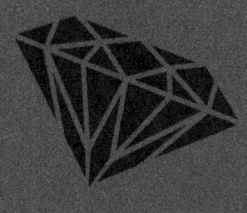

Prompt 39

Date: _____

How do I grow my wealth without losing my values?

next steps

Only say yes to money that feels good to earn.

Prompt 40

Date: _____

What financial risk am I ready to take?

next steps

Write it down and take one first move toward it.

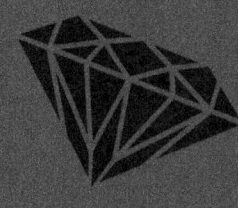

Prompt 41

Date: _____

How do I stay motivated when money feels slow?

---

next steps

Look at how far you've come, not how far to go.

Prompt 42

Date: _____

What's one way I could earn more money?

next steps

Brainstorm five quick ideas and circle the easiest one.

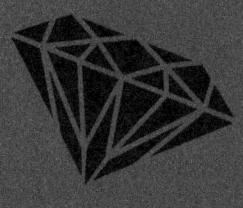

Prompt 43

Date: _____

What's my vision for a wealthy life?

next steps

Describe one part of it you can start living now.

Prompt 44

Date: _____

What's my biggest money win this month?

next steps

Write it down and celebrate it — no matter the size.

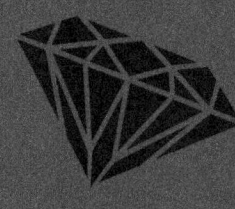

Prompt 45

Date: _____

How can I use my skills to make more money?

next steps

List your top three skills and one way to monetize each.

Prompt 46

Date: _____

What's my plan for handling money stress?

next steps

Create one go-to habit that calms you fast.

Prompt 47

Date: _____

What money habit do I want to build this month?

---

next steps

Start tracking it daily — one small win at a time.

Prompt 48

Date: _____

How do I measure my money progress?

next steps

Pick one number to track that actually motivates you.

Prompt 49

Date: _____

What's my plan for surprise expenses?

---

next steps

Decide on a backup plan before you need it.

Prompt 50

Date: _____

What money boundary matters most and how will I protect it?

next steps

Honor it by saying no once this week when it counts.

Reflection
CHECK-IN #2

Take a minute to reflect on the last 25 prompts. What did you learn about yourself & your relationship with money?

WHAT'S YOUR FOCUS RIGHT NOW?

ACTION STEPS

1

2

3

REALIZATIONS

Wealth Notes

Wealth Notes

Wealth Notes

Wealth Notes

Wealth Notes

UNLOCKING

UNLOCK THE PATTERNS THAT SHAPE YOUR FINANCIAL REALITY.

Prompt 51

Date: _____

What money story am I ready to rewrite?

---

next steps

Write the new story you want to believe instead.

Prompt 52

Date: _____

What money story did I grow up with that doesn't help me now?

next steps

Thank it for getting you here, then let it go.

Prompt 53

Date: _____

What belief about money needs to change?

next steps

Replace it with one that actually supports your goals.

Prompt 54

Date: _____

What money myth do I know isn't true anymore?

next steps

Say the truth out loud — and live from that.

Prompt 55

Date: _____

What's my biggest mindset block with money right now?

next steps

Call it out and remind yourself it's not a fact.

Prompt 56

Date: _____

What money fear am I done giving power to?

next steps

Write the fear once, then cross it out.

Prompt 57

Date: _____

What bold money move have I been putting off?

---

next steps

Take the first small step toward it today.

Prompt 58

Date: _____

Where am I still playing small with money?

next steps

Choose one area to show up bigger.

Prompt 59

Date: _____

Where do I still feel lack with money and why?

next steps

Look for proof that you already have enough.

Prompt 60

Date: _____

How can I choose trust instead of fear with money?

next steps

Do one thing today from confidence, not worry.

Prompt 61

Date: _____

What fears show up when I want more money?

next steps

Write them down and challenge each one with truth.

Prompt 62

Date: _____

What habits or patterns keep me stuck financially?

next steps

Pick one to stop and replace it with something better.

QUOTE

Your Self-confidence is the key to unlocking your full potential. Believe in your abilities and there will be no limit to what you can achieve.

QUOTE

Prompt 63

Date: _____

What proof do I already have that I'm abundant?

next steps

Write three examples that show money supports you.

Prompt 64

Date: _____

What does my next-level wealthy self believe about money?

next steps

Write one belief and practice thinking it all day.

Prompt 65

Date: _____

How can I make peace with my money past?

next steps

Forgive yourself and move forward with what you've learned.

Prompt 66

Date: _____

How do I bounce back when money things go wrong?

next steps

Remember what worked last time — repeat that.

Prompt 67

Date: _____

How can I release fear and give myself room to grow?

next steps

Replace fear with action. Even one small move counts.

Prompt 68

Date: _____

What's the biggest money lesson I've learned so far?

next steps

Write it down and don't forget it.

Prompt 69

Date: _____

What's one money habit I'm ready to drop?

next steps

Replace it with one that feels good and smart.

Prompt 70

Date: _____

How can I celebrate money wins without guilt?

---

next steps

Enjoy it fully — no explaining, no shrinking.

Prompt 71

Date: _____

What's one money win that came from a mistake?

next steps

Write the lesson that turned it into progress.

Prompt 72

Date: _____

What money lesson am I grateful for?

next steps

Thank that lesson — it made you stronger.

Prompt 73

Date: _____

How can I act like my wealthiest self today?

next steps

Make one confident decision she'd already make.

Prompt 74

Date: _____

How can I create a daily routine that brings in more money?

next steps

Add one small habit that keeps you in motion

Prompt 75

Date: _____

What's one money thought I can shift today?

next steps

Catch it, flip it, and repeat the new one all day.

Reflection
CHECK-IN #3

Take a minute to reflect on the last 25 prompts. What did you learn about yourself & your relationship with money?

WHAT'S YOUR FOCUS RIGHT NOW?

ACTION STEPS

1

2

3

REALIZATIONS

Wealth Notes

Wealth Notes

Wealth Notes

Wealth Notes

Wealth Notes

REFLECTION

REFLECT, RECEIVE, AND MAKE SPACE FOR MORE.

Prompt 76

Date: _____

How do I feel about money right now?

next steps

Be honest. Awareness is where change starts.

Prompt 77

Date: _____

What money wins have I had lately?

next steps

Write them down. Give yourself credit.

Prompt 78

Date: _____

What money habits do I want my kids or others to learn from me

next steps

Keep showing them what's possible by example.

Prompt 79

Date: _____

What money story do I want my future self to remember?

next steps

Write it as if you already lived it.

Prompt 80

Date: _____

What money lessons am I most thankful for?

next steps

Appreciate what taught you to grow.

Prompt 81

Date: _____

What's one thing I'm grateful I can pay for today?

next steps

Say thank you while you spend it.

Prompt 82

Date: _____

How do I celebrate when money comes in?

next steps

Find a small ritual that feels good and repeat it.

Prompt 83

Date: _____

How do I celebrate the small wins with money?

next steps

Notice one today and actually pause to feel it.

Prompt 84

Date: _____

How does being wealthy help me give more?

next steps

See giving as proof of overflow, not loss.

Prompt 85

Date: _____

Where does generosity fit in my money goals?

next steps

Give from joy, not guilt.

Prompt 86

Date: _____

How can I be generous with money in a way that feels right?

---

next steps

Give what feels aligned, not what drains you.

Prompt 87

Date: _____

What habits or patterns around money have changed?

---

next steps

Acknowledge how far you've already come.

Prompt 88

Date: _____

How do I stay calm when money feels tight?

next steps

Breathe and remember — this moment isn't forever.

INSPIRATION QUOTE

"Confidence isn't build by waiting for proof. It's built by choosing to trust yourself before the evidence ever shows up."

Christina Ostroski

Prompt 89

Date: _____

How can I turn a current money challenge into a win?

next steps

Look for the lesson or the opportunity in it.

Prompt 90

Date: _____

What's my relationship with debt and how can I improve it?

next steps

Shift from shame to strategy. Make a plan.

Prompt 91

Date: _____

How can I make my money work smarter for me?

next steps

Find one place to simplify or automate.

Prompt 92

Date: _____

What money fears have I already let go of?

next steps

Write them down as proof of growth.

Prompt 93

Date: _____

How can I forgive myself for past money mistakes?

next steps

You learned. That's the win. Move forward clean.

Prompt 94

Date: _____

What old patterns no longer control me?

next steps

Celebrate that version of you being gone.

Prompt 95

Date: _____

How do I want to teach others about money?

next steps

Lead with what you've learned, not what you fear.

Prompt 96

Date: _____

How do I keep my motivation on tough money days?

next steps

Remember your why and keep moving anyway.

Prompt 97

Date: _____

What money win came from a mistake I made?

next steps

Turn that story into proof you can figure it out.

Prompt 98

Date: _____

How can I be more patient with my finances?

next steps

Trust the process — growth takes time.

Prompt 99

Date: _____

How can I create cash flow that feels easy?

next steps

Do what feels natural, not forced.

Prompt 100

Date: _____

What's my new money identity statement?

next steps

Write it like a declaration and believe every word.

Prompt 101

Date: _____

How do I live as the woman who already has everything she wants?

---

next steps

Own it now. Start living like it's already yours, speak it, wear it, walk it, and let your choices match the woman you've become.

Reflection CHECK-IN #4

Take a minute to reflect on the last 25 prompts. What did you learn about yourself & your relationship with money?

WHAT'S YOUR FOCUS RIGHT NOW?

ACTION STEPS

1

2

3

REALIZATIONS

Wealth Notes

Wealth Notes

Wealth Notes

Wealth Notes

Wealth Notes

Wealth Notes

Wealth Practice

INTEGRATION WORKSHEETS

Wealth CHECK-IN

You've done the work, shifted your mindset, and rewritten your money story one page at a time.

Now it's time to see the change in motion. This check-in is your reflection point, a moment to celebrate how much you've grown and the wealth identity you've stepped into.

Read your first check-in again. Feel the difference in your words, your energy, and your confidence. This is your evolution in real time.

- How has my relationship with money changed?
- What new beliefs feel natural now?
- What money wins have I created?
- What old patterns no longer run my life?
- What's my next-level money goal?

Wealth Identity Statement

I NOW SEE MYELF AS _____

Wealth Notes

Money Mindset REFLECTIONS

WHAT'S THE BIGGEST TAKEAWAY ABOUT HOW YOU THINK OR FEEL ABOUT MONEY?

Money Mindset REFLECTIONS

WHAT FRUSTRATES ME ABOUT MONEY?

WHAT DO I LOVE ABOUT MONEY?

Money Mindset
REFLECTIONS

ONE THING THAT'S BEEN WORKING WELL

ONE THING THAT NEEDS ADJUSTING

ONE THING TO FOCUS ON NEXT

Wealth Framework
6 STEP ROADMAP

YOUR STEP-BY-STEP PATH TO EMBODY, ALIGN, AND ATTRACT WEALTH IN EVERY AREA OF YOUR LIFE.

W-WITHIN
Start by connecting to the version of you who already has it all. Your inner world sets the tone for your outer results.

E-ELICIT
Bring forward the emotions that match your goals. Feel it first, then watch your reality catch up.

A-ATTRACT
Align your thoughts, energy, and actions so money naturally flows your way.

L-LANGUAGE
Your words shape your wealth. Speak abundance and watch your world respond.

T-THOUGHT CATCHING
Notice the thoughts that limit you and replace them with ones that move you forward.

H-HEAL
Release old stories, shame and blocks so you can receive with ease and confidence.

Wealth Awareness CHECKLIST

W — CONNECT TO YOUR WEALTHIEST SELF ☐
Check in with how aligned you feel with the version of you who has it all.

E — FEEL IT FIRST ☐
Notice if your emotions match the wealth you're calling in today.

A — ALIGN YOUR ENERGY ☐
Notice if your thoughts, energy, and actions are moving you closer to what you want or pulling you away.

L — SPEAK LIKE WEALTH ☐
Listen to your words - are you affirming abundance or doudt?

T — CHECK YOUR THOUGHTS ☐
Pay attention to where you slip into lack and reframe it.

H — RELEASE AND RESET ☐
Acknowledge what you're ready to let go of so more can flow in.

Breakthrough
JOURNAL PAGE

WHAT GOAL ARE YOU WORKING TOWARDS?

_____

_____

_____

_____

_____

_____

ACTION STEPS

1

2

3

START DATE: **DEADLINE:**   **MARK COMPLETE:**

Wealth Assessment
RATE YES OR NO

01	DO I ACTUALLY THINK LIKE SOEONE WHO'S WEALTHY?	YES ☐	NO ☐
02	DO I TRUST MONEY TO KEEP SHOWING UP FOR ME?	YES ☐	NO ☐
03	DO I SPEAK ABOUT MONEY WITH POWER, NOT GUILT?	YES ☐	NO ☐
04	DO I CATCH MYSELF WHEN I SLIP INOT LACK?	YES ☐	NO ☐
05	DO I MAKE CHOICES LIKE SOMEONE WHO ALREADY HAS WHAT THEY WANT?	YES ☐	NO ☐
06	DO I ALLOW MONEY TO FEEL EASY OR SOMETHING CHASE?	YES ☐	NO ☐
07	DO I CELEBRATE MONEY NO MATTER HOW IT COMES IN?	YES ☐	NO ☐

Wealth Assessment
POLAR OPOSITES

I SEE MONEY AS HARD TO EARN — EASY TO ATTRACT
0 1 2 3 4 5 6 7 8 9 10

I FEEL NERVOUS WHEN SPENDING — CONFIDENT WHEN SPENDING
0 1 2 3 4 5 6 7 8 9 10

I BELIEVE WEALTH IS FOR OTHERS — I BELEIVE WEALTH IS FOR ME
0 1 2 3 4 5 6 7 8 9 10

I WORK TO GET BY — I WORK TO CREATE MORE THAN ENOUGH
0 1 2 3 4 5 6 7 8 9 10

THERE'S NEVER ENOUGH — THERE'S ALWAYS MORE COMING
0 1 2 3 4 5 6 7 8 9 10

I FEEL GUILT AROUND MONEY — I FEEL GRATITUDE AROUND MONEY
0 1 2 3 4 5 6 7 8 9 10

I ACT FROM FEAR — I ACT FROM CONFIDENCE
0 1 2 3 4 5 6 7 8 9 10

Frequently Asked QUESTIONS

Q Why does it feel like money disappears as soon as I get it?

It's usually because deep down you're expecting it to. When you believe money never sticks around, you'll always find a way to make that true. Change the expectation, and the pattern changes.

Q How do I stop stressing about money all the time?

By getting control of what you can control and letting go of what you can't. Write down what you earn, spend, and owe. Make one small move you can act on right now, even if it's tiny. Check in with your money once a week so it feels manageable, not mysterious.

Q How do I start thinking like someone who actually has their finances together?

You start thinking like someone who has their finances together by deciding you're that person right now. You stop avoiding your money, you stop judging yourself for what you did before, and you start paying attention to what's actually coming in and going out. The more you take ownership, the more in control you feel.

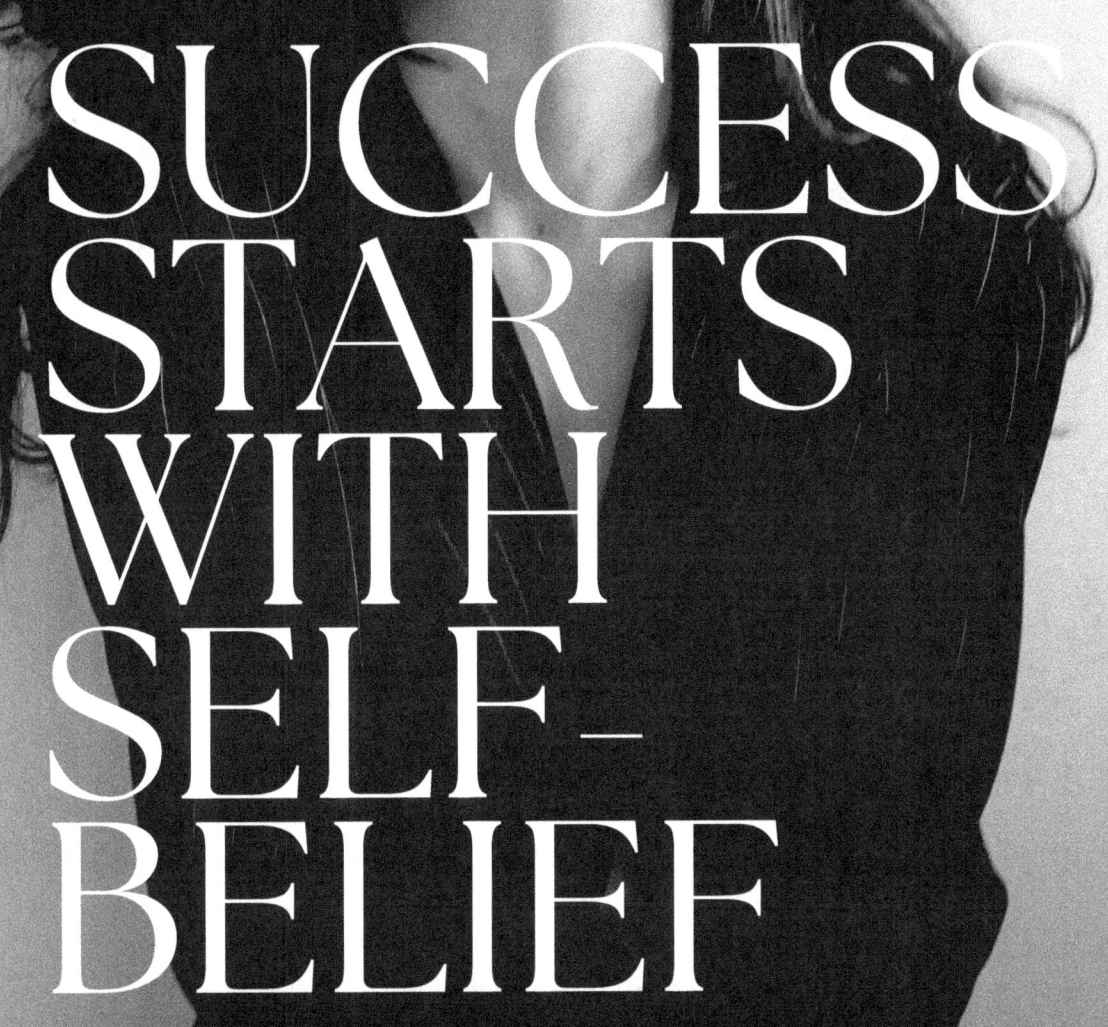

Welcome Friend!
I'M CHRISTINA

An NLP Trainer, Wealth and Mindset Expert, and founder of The Wealth Method™, a framework designed to help redefine wealth from the inside out. Her approach blends neuroscience, energetics, psychology, metaphysics, quantum physics, and ancient wisdom into practical, powerful teachings that go beyond trends.

A respected leader in personal development and wealth mindset, her journey from pregnant teen to acclaimed NLP Trainer, Master Mindset and Success Coach, Hypnotherapist, EFT Practitioner, and Astrologer proves that transformation is possible for anyone ready to rewrite their story.

Follow Christina to work with her, read more, or learn about upcoming books, programs, and events.

@IAMCHRISTINAOSTORKSI

ALIGNED LUXURY

Luxury isn't about designer bags, five-star hotels, or expensive things. It's how you move when you know your worth. When you stop working for approval and start owning who you are. When gratitude and desire can live in the same moment.

It's not about proving anything. It's not about being better than anyone. It's about choosing to live in a way that feels rich in mind, body, and soul, even before the money shows up.

Luxury is not earned. It's embodied. It becomes available the moment you stop chasing and start aligning.

It's not something you buy. It's something you become.

READY TO GO DEEPER?

Start your full transformation with **The Sequence to Aligned Wealth**, the book that started it. Find it online or at your local bookstores where available.

GET IN TOUCH

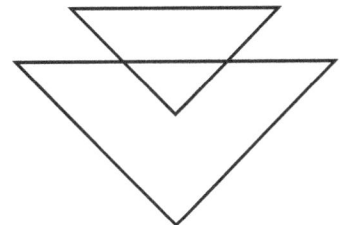

THANK YOU FOR YOUR SUPPORT

The 101 Money Mindset Prompt Book was created by Christina Ostroski.

Scan the QR code below to connect with me on social media and stay updated on new releases.

Or search Christina Ostroski on Amazon to explore my full book collection.

Follow me on Social Media:
@iamchristinaostroski

THINK WEALTH. SPEAK MONEY. BE RICH.

Wealth Notes

www.ingramcontent.com/pod-product-compliance
Lightning Source LLC
Chambersburg PA
CBHW082216090526
44584CB00025BA/3729